STARK COUNTY DISTRICT LIBRARY JUL 2019

W9-ALM-804

DISCARDED

THE IMPORTANCE OF PLANTS TO LIFE ON EARTH

YEA JEE BAE

Britannica®
Educational Publishing

IN ASSOCIATION WITH

ROSEN
EDUCATIONAL SERVICES

Published in 2019 by Britannica Educational Publishing (a trademark of Encyclopædia Britannica, Inc.) in association with The Rosen Publishing Group, Inc.
29 East 21st Street, New York, NY 10010

Copyright © 2019 The Rosen Publishing Group, Inc. and Encyclopædia Britannica, Inc. Encyclopædia Britannica, Britannica, and the Thistle logo are registered trademarks of Encyclopædia Britannica, Inc. All rights reserved.

Distributed exclusively by Rosen Publishing.
To see additional Britannica Educational Publishing titles, go to rosenpublishing.com.

First Edition

Britannica Educational Publishing
J.E. Luebering: Executive Director, Core Editorial
Mary Rose McCudden: Editor, Britannica Student Encyclopedia

Rosen Publishing
Louise Eaton: Editor
Nelson Sá: Art Director
Nicole Russo-Duca: Series Designer/Book Layout
Cindy Reiman: Photography Manager
Ellina Litmanovich: Photo Researcher

Library of Congress Cataloging-in-Publication Data

Names: Bae, Yea Jee, author.
Title: The importance of plants to life on earth / Yea Jee Bae.
Description: New York : Britannica Educational Publishing, in Association with Rosen Educational Services, 2019. | Series: Let's find out! Plants | Includes bibliographical references and index. | Audience: Grades 1–4.
Identifiers: LCCN 2017048762| ISBN 9781538301975 (library bound) | ISBN 9781538301982 (pbk.) | ISBN 9781538301999 (6 pack)
Subjects: LCSH: Plants—Juvenile literature. | Plants, Useful—Juvenile literature. | Food chains (Ecology)—Juvenile literature.
Classification: LCC QK49 .B14494 2019 | DDC 581—dc23
LC record available at https://lccn.loc.gov/2017048762

Manufactured in the United States of America

Photo credits: Cover, interior pages background Anna Om/Shutterstock.com; pp. 4, 15, 25 © AdstockRF; p. 5 © James P. Rowan; pp. 6, 8 © Encyclopædia Britannica, Inc.; p. 7 Quality Stock Arts/Shutterstock.com; p. 9 Preeda340/Shutterstock.com; p. 10 Daniel Tadevosyan/Shutterstock.com; p. 11 kramar89/Shutterstock.com; p. 12 donyanedomam/Fotolia; p. 13 Alex Yeung/Fotolia; p. 14 kikisora/Fotolia; p. 16 franco lucato/Shutterstock.com; p. 17 Corbis; p. 18 Xico Putini; p. 19 Stuart Taylor/Fotolia; p. 20 Luis Echeverri Urrea/Shutterstock.com; p. 21 Georgiy Pashin/Fotolia; p. 22 By Andrew Koturanov/Shutterstock.com; p. 23 © Walter Chandoha; p. 24 © Comstock Images/Jupiterimages; p. 26 Oren Sarid/Fotolia; p. 27 Skinfaxi/Shutterstock.com; p. 28 Andrew Orlemann/Fotolia; p. 29 David Fine/FEMA.

CONTENTS

LIFE STARTS WITH PLANTS

From tiny patches of grass clinging to cliffs to giant trees as tall as towers, plants are found all over the world. If there is sunlight, water, and air, plants can grow—and some plants can exist with even less. More than three hundred thousand different species of plants have been discovered. Scientists believe that there are

This juniper tree, in Yosemite National Park in central California, is able to grow on a rocky cliff.

a great many more species that are still unidentified. New plant species continue to be found in less explored areas of the world, such as tropical forests.

THINK ABOUT IT

New plants are often found in tropical forests. Why do you think tropical forests have so many different plant species?

Most plants are rooted in one place and are not able to move around. A stiff material called cellulose makes up their cell walls and gives them shape. Through a process called photosynthesis, plants create their own food. In many, many ways, humans and animals depend on plants. Without plants, life as we know it could not survive on Earth.

Many animals, like these impalas in Kenya, graze on plants for their primary source of food.

ENERGY SOURCE

Plants are autotrophs. This means that they create their own energy. They do this through photosynthesis, a process that requires sunlight, chlorophyll, water, and carbon dioxide. Chlorophyll is a substance naturally found inside green plants. It allows plants to absorb energy from the sun. With this energy, plants

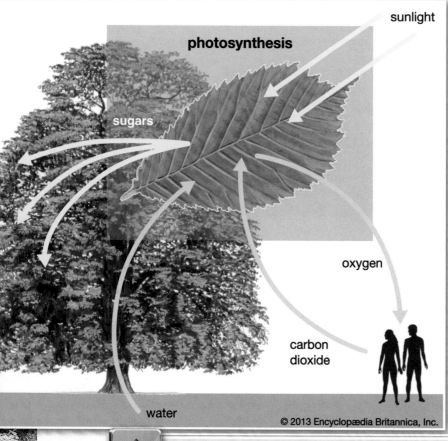

photosynthesis

sunlight

sugars

oxygen

carbon dioxide

water

© 2013 Encyclopædia Britannica, Inc.

Plants use photosynthesis to transform light energy from the sun into chemical energy.

Most plants contain chlorophyll. This natural substance is what gives green plants their color.

change the water in the soil and the carbon dioxide in the air into oxygen and nutrients. The oxygen is released into the air. Some of the nutrients are used, and the rest are stored.

Photosynthesis is vital to life on Earth. Without photosynthesis, there would be no plants, and without plants, there would be no food for humans and animals. As producers that make their own food, plants are the start of most food chains. This means that nearly all living things depend on plants for energy.

VOCABULARY
Autotrophs are organisms that can make their own food from substances that do not come from other living things.

THE AIR WE BREATHE

All living things need air to survive. Air is a mixture of the gases of different chemical elements. Of these gases, oxygen and nitrogen are the most common. They make up 99 percent of the air. Oxygen is important because humans and animals need to breathe it to live.

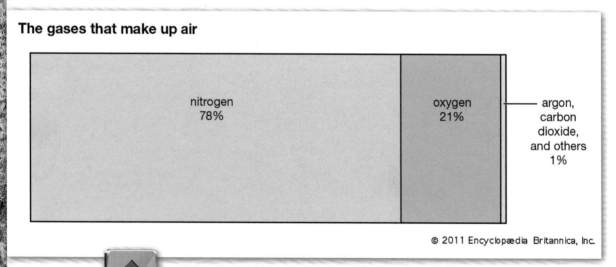

The gases that make up air

nitrogen
78%

oxygen
21%

argon, carbon dioxide, and others 1%

© 2011 Encyclopædia Britannica, Inc.

This diagram shows the composition of air, which is made up of many gases. There is more nitrogen in the air than any other gas.

Most of the oxygen in the atmosphere comes from plants. When humans and other animals breathe, we take in oxygen and release carbon dioxide. If there is too much carbon dioxide and not enough oxygen in the air, it can become harmful to our bodies. However, plants take in the carbon dioxide during photosynthesis and convert it to oxygen we can breathe. This forms a cycle where the carbon dioxide and oxygen in the atmosphere are constantly being used and replaced.

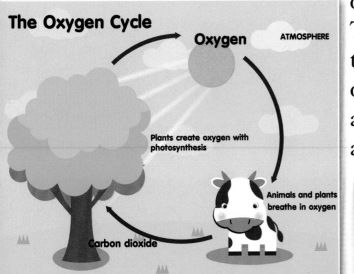

The Oxygen Cycle

Oxygen   ATMOSPHERE

Plants create oxygen with photosynthesis

Animals and plants breathe in oxygen

Carbon dioxide

With the help of plants, oxygen and carbon dioxide repeatedly circulate in what is known as the oxygen cycle.

PROTECTING NATURE

Plants help the environment and are an important part of ecosystems. Mosses, tree roots, and other plants work to break down rocks. This enriches the soil by adding minerals to it and also stabilizes the soil. Dead plant matter, such as fallen leaves from trees, also enriches the soil. Soil is also protected from erosion by plants. If plants did not hold soil in place with their roots, it could easily be blown or washed away by wind and rain.

◀◀ Plants can erode rocks. This improves the soil, since the minerals from the rock go into the ground.

Ecosystems are made up of all the living things and nonliving materials in an area. They usually contain many kinds of life interacting with each other and their surroundings.

Plants conserve natural resources as well. In addition to preventing erosion, they control the level and quality of water by taking in and evaporating water. They help maintain a healthy atmosphere. They also cycle nutrients and absorb minerals from the soil.

Many plants have long roots that grip the soil tightly and prevent it from being swept away.

PROVIDING SHELTER

For many living things, plants provide shelter from the weather and protection from predators. Many birds make their nests in trees, as do bees. Staying in trees offers both cover and distance from dangers. For this reason, some animals, like apes, will build themselves temporary shelters up in trees to sleep in so they are safely off the ground. However, large plants like trees are not the only source of shelter for animals. Even small plants

By hanging in trees, this orangutan can find protection from predators on the ground.

COMPARE AND CONTRAST

How are the shelters that animals make different from the shelters that people make? How are they the same?

can shield tiny insects from rain with their leaves. Low bushes provide hiding places for small animals like mice and rabbits.

Plants also provide the raw materials for many shelters. Birds use twigs and other plant matter to build their nests. All around the world, humans use wood from trees to build their houses. Other plant materials are also sometimes found in human dwellings. For example, the roofs of simple houses or shelters can be made from straw or leaves.

Birds commonly build nests in trees to raise their young. The height and surrounding branches and leaves provide shelter.

13

Food for Consumers

Plants provide food for all other consumers in a food chain, either directly or indirectly. For example, a rabbit eats plants. That is direct consumption, and the rabbit can be called a primary consumer of plants. If a fox eats the rabbit, it is indirectly consuming plants, which makes it a secondary consumer.

Humans are both primary and secondary consumers of plants. They are primary consumers when they eat plants directly. They are secondary consumers when they eat animals that ate plants.

These Japanese beetles are eating a leaf. This is direct consumption, making them primary consumers of plants.

Humans eat many fruits and vegetables, which are parts of plants. They can be found for sale at markets.

Plants contain nutrients that we need in order to be healthy. In North America, grains and legumes are our greatest sources of plant-based food. We also use seasonings, many of which come from plants, to flavor and preserve our food. Pepper and nutmeg are derived from dried fruits, and herbs like thyme and sage come from leaves. Many of our drinks come from plants as well. Coffee and tea are made by using hot water to brew plant ingredients, and juices come from fruits.

Think About It

What animals besides humans are both primary and secondary consumers?

GROWING CROPS

Long ago, humans did not live in permanent settlements. People would go out to places like forests to find edible plants where they grew. Today, most of the plants that people eat have been intentionally raised as crops instead of gathered in the wild. Humans depend on crops to feed livestock such as cows and pigs, too. Farming is mainly a family-run business in most countries. In more-developed places, there are many large company-run farms that specialize in one type of crop.

Farming is also important for the economy. To earn money, farmers depend on growing cash crops.

People around the world living in small communities may go out to gather their food.

Governments often have programs to help farmers so that they can afford to grow the crops that feed other people. In the United States and other developed countries, farmers often produce more food than is needed in the immediate area. Surplus crops are sold around the world. This helps people have access to all kinds of food. For example, people in cold climates can buy oranges to eat, even though oranges can only grow in places with warmer climates.

VOCABULARY

Cash crops are crops that farmers grow to sell rather than to use themselves.

The crops harvested on a farm, like these tea leaves grown in Thailand, can be distributed all over the world.

17

PLANTS IN INDUSTRY

Many of the materials used in industry come from plants. Trees provide a wide variety of these resources, such as wood, cork, rubber, resins, and important oils. Cellulose from plants is a basic ingredient of many products. It is used to create certain plastics, as well as synthetic substitutes for natural fibers, glass, leather, jewels, and metal. Plant material rich in cellulose is also used to make pulp for paper.

VOCABULARY

Synthetic means produced artificially.

Castor-oil plants provide an oil that is used in food additives, many modern medicines, and cosmetic products.

Rubber trees are harvested by making cuts in their bark to let out latex fluid. This process is called "tapping."

Some plant crops have many industrial uses. Corn can be processed to make a synthetic fiber. Other corn products are used in plastics, textile colors, and printing inks. Cornstarch is used to toughen and glaze paper, textiles, and fabrics. Soybeans have versatile uses as well. Soybean oil is used as an ingredient in paints, adhesives, insect sprays, fire extinguisher fluids, and more.

Plant Fuel

At the beginning of the twenty-first century, almost 90 percent of the world's energy supply was made up of fossil fuels. Coal is the most common and widely used fossil fuel. It was formed from plants that grew in humid, swampy regions millions of years ago. When dead plant matter fell into a swamp, it formed a thick layer at the swamp bottom. Over time, sediment covered and pressed down on this **decaying** plant layer. The plant layer became peat. The

> **VOCABULARY**
> **Decaying** means breaking down.

Castor oil comes from the seeds of the castor-oil plant. It can be used in the production of some kinds of fuel.

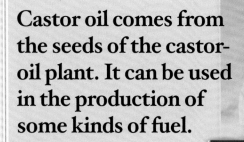

peat then turned into different types of soft and hard coal depending on how much heat and pressure it was exposed to.

Fossil fuels are used in factories, homes, and transportation. Other types of fuel are widely used as well. Wood is a popular source of fuel for heat, and peat is common in Ireland and certain other countries in Northern Europe. Charcoal is formed from partially burned wood. It is used for cooking food outdoors and for some industrial purposes.

Charcoal contains carbon. When charcoal is burned, it doesn't produce smoke.

Medicine from Plants

For thousands of years people have turned to plants to treat their pains and injuries. Ancient cultures had healers who were experts on plants. Many plants discovered by these early peoples are still used today.

Since ancient times, people have chewed willow bark to find relief from pain.

The bark from willow trees like these contains a chemical that helps relieve pain.

The bark contains a chemical similar to aspirin. Quinine, found in the bark of the South American cinchona tree, is used to fight a disease called malaria. Digitalis, found in foxglove leaves, is used to treat heart disease.

Many of the drugs that are created today in laboratories originally came from plants. New substances are still being discovered in plants. Vincristine is a medicine used to treat certain types of cancer. It was found in a type of periwinkle plant that is native to the African island of Madagascar. Plants are also a valuable source of many vitamins.

COMPARE AND CONTRAST

How has the way we use plants for medical purposes changed from the past?

Important medicinal substances have been discovered from common plants like the periwinkle.

23

Plants are Everywhere

Plants are an incredibly versatile resource. Plant-made materials and products can be found almost anywhere in all different forms. Many clothes are made from plant materials. Cotton is the main plant used in clothing production. Linen, another common fabric for clothes, comes from the flax plant. Artificial textiles like rayon are made mostly from cellulose fibers, which are found in the cell walls of plants. These fibers can be combined and woven together to create fabrics. Dyes to change the color of these fabrics are also often made from plants.

Because of its widespread use, cotton was a major crop of the American South for many years.

THINK ABOUT IT

Products made from plants don't always look like they came from plants. What are some other plant-made products that you can think of?

Cloth made from plant fibers is also used in furniture, along with wood. Wallpaper is made from plant pulp that has been pressed and dried into a thin sheet. Other products that come from plants include turpentine, cocoa butter, and makeup.

The dyes produced in this Moroccan tannery's dyeing pits can be used to color fabrics.

Natural Beauty

Plants are important for many practical reasons, but they are also simply beautiful to look at. People plant flowers, bushes, and trees in their yards and gardens for decoration. Gardens have been around since ancient times. At first gardens were only useful for providing herbs and other foods. Later, people began to grow flower gardens for the simple purpose of beauty.

Plants are common in people's homes and offices and in public spaces. They have become a part of human

The main purpose of the Butchart Gardens in Victoria, British Columbia, Canada, is to display the beauty of flowers.

Bouquets of flowers like this are common gifts for celebrations, such as a birthday or an anniversary.

culture. People give one another flowers as gifts, such as to celebrate a performance. Flowers can also be used to express sympathy, such as at a funeral. Apart from being attractive, plants can also relax people and help reduce stress.

COMPARE AND CONTRAST

Rural areas tend to have more plants and greenery than developed city landscapes. How do you think people's moods might be affected by the presence or lack of plants in their surroundings?

THREATS TO PLANTS

People have been cutting down trees for thousands of years. Today deforestation, or cutting down a great many trees, is common. It can cause permanent damage to the local environment. For example, animals that live in forests lose their habitat when the trees are cut down. Also, trees and other plants, rooted in the ground, keep the soil in place. When too many plants are lost, the rain can easily wash away the soil. Additionally, trees are needed to capture carbon dioxide and produce oxygen.

Fire can quickly spread through a forest, burning trees, grasses, and habitats. The effects from the destruction are long-lasting.

Sometimes people burn trees to clear land for farming. That creates another problem. The burning trees add more carbon dioxide to the air. The extra carbon dioxide contributes to global warming. Global warming is an increase in Earth's average surface temperature. The warming climate has started to affect the life cycle of some plants. For example, trees have begun to produce leaves earlier in the spring. Droughts and floods have also increased. As climate change continues, biologists estimate that many plants will face an increased risk of extinction, or dying out.

Think About It

Plants are essential for life on our planet. What can we do to help protect plants?

After severe rain storms in Nashville, Tennessee, in 2010, the Cumberland River flooded its banks, causing widespread damage.

GLOSSARY

atmosphere The whole mass of air surrounding Earth.

carbon dioxide A gas in the atmosphere that is necessary for life on Earth.

climate The average weather conditions of a particular place or region over a period of years.

convert To change from one substance, form, use, or unit to another.

deforestation The action or process of clearing an area of forests.

edible Fit or safe to be eaten.

enrich To make more fertile and desirable.

erosion The process of being worn away by the action of water, wind, or glacial ice.

fertile Suited for growing crops.

fibers Thin strands of material.

food chain The order in which living things depend on each other for food.

fossil fuel A kind of fuel, such as coal, petroleum (oil), and natural gas, that is the remains of organisms that lived long ago.

humid Damp and moist.

legume Plants such as peas, peanuts, and beans that produce pods.

nutrient Substance that the body needs to grow and maintain itself.

sediment Material, such as stones and sand, deposited by water, wind, and glaciers.

species A specific type of living thing. Human beings are a species.

surplus More than what is required or necessary.

textile Woven or knitted cloth.

versatile Able to do many different things.

vital Very important.

For More Information

Books

Bow, James. *Earth's Climate Change: Carbon Dioxide Overload.* New York, NY: Crabtree Publishing Company, 2015.

Dickmann, Nancy. *Plant Structures.* New York, NY: Cavendish Square Publishing, 2015.

Long, Erin. *Plants and Their Environments.* New York, NY: PowerKids Press, 2017.

Machajewski, Sarah. *We Need Plants.* New York, NY: PowerKids Press, 2016.

Owen, Ruth. *How Do Plants Make Their Own Food?* New York, NY: PowerKids Press, 2014.

Zuchora-Walske, Christine. *Photosynthesis.* Minneapolis, MN: Abdo Publishing Company, 2014.

Websites

Ag for Kids
http://agforkids.com/home/home?CSRF_TOKEN=1b8f8dfd9084d101 61c2ca45b8b6799a21fa50b6

MBG Net
http://www.mbgnet.net/bioplants/earth.html

Plant-Talk
http://www.plant-talk.org/news/why-conserve-plants.htm

United States Botanic Garden
https://www.usbg.gov
Facebook, Instagram: @usbotanicgarden

INDEX